North-West England

LANDSCAPES

Simon Kirwan

Text: Liam Kirwan

MYRIAD

LONDON

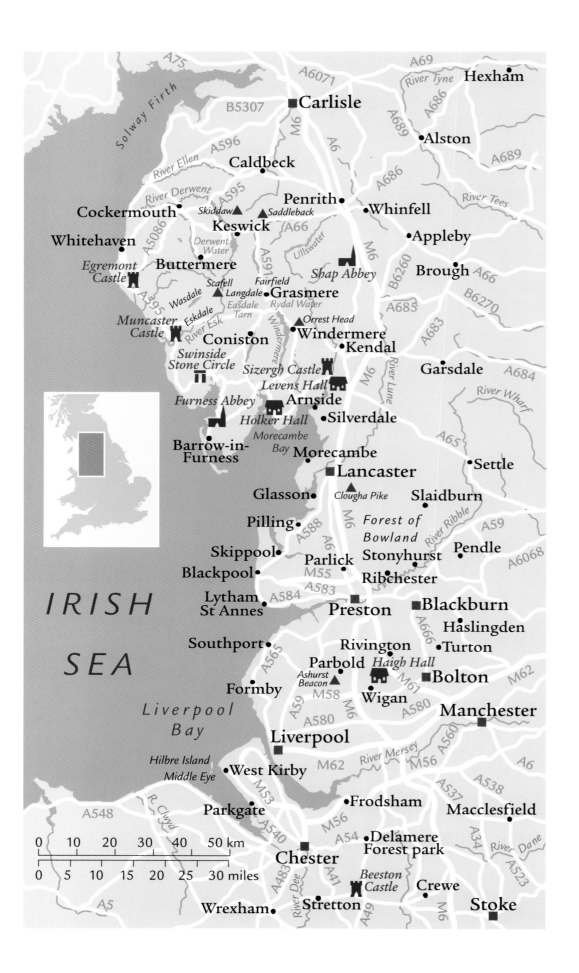

First published in 2007
by Myriad Books Limited,
35 Bishopsthorpe Road,
London SE26 4PA

Photographs copyright
© Simon Kirwan
Text copyright
© Liam Kirwan

Liam Kirwan has asserted
his right under the Copyright,
Designs and Patents Act 1998 to
be identified as the author of
this work.

ISBN 1 84746 012 7
EAN 978 1 84746 012 7

Designed by Jerry Goldie
Graphic Design
Printed in China

www.myriadbooks.com

Title page: Clougha Pike;
opposite: the beach at Blackpool

Contents

North-West England Landscapes

NORTH-WEST ENGLAND covers a vast area stretching from the Cheshire plain in the south to the Cumbrian fells in the north, taking in the Wirral, Lancashire, the Fylde, and the urban conurbations of Merseyside and Greater Manchester along the way. Connecting it all is water – the outstretched finger of the Wirral peninsula has the river Dee to its west, and to the east the river Mersey links Liverpool and Manchester. The inland region of east Lancashire is, like the Lake District, punctuated by a combination of natural lakes and man-made reservoirs, constructed to provide water for the emerging towns and cities which proliferated after the industrial revolution. The west coast looks out to the Irish Sea and is famous for its sunsets, so much so that England's greatest landscape painter, JMW Turner, toured north Lancashire in the late 18th century and produced celebrated paintings of the Lune Valley and Lancaster Sands.

I was born on the outskirts of Liverpool, a stone's throw from the mouth of the Mersey as it flows into the Irish Sea. In those days pollution was rife, and caring for the environment was not widely understood or thought necessary. Nowadays, thankfully, things are different. Recently I walked along the vast beach at Southport, north of Formby Point, where the outgoing tide exposes a mile or more of sand. The shoreline was marked not by the empty bottles and plastic detritus that used to mar the sands. Instead, starfish and razor shells lay about in profusion, visible evidence of the concerted efforts that have been made to reclaim the waters from the century of domestic and industrial effluent that previously polluted this coastline. Further north, the sprawling estuary of the Ribble is one of Europe's most important regions for over-wintering wading birds and wildfowl, supporting over a quarter of a million birds each year.

Southport, where I have lived for the last 20 years, is set amidst a flat landscape. But from the end of the Victorian pier, which juts out for a mile across the open sand and sea, it is possible to view many hills and mountains – much of the hilly uplands of north-west England, from the Lakeland fells of Cumbria to the north, the rounded hills of the Forest of Bowland to the north-east and, looking south-west, the Clwydian Hills along the border of north Wales. Here you can see the connection between water and land which is such a feature of this part of Britain. From those same uplands the sea, or at least a lake or reservoir, is almost always in sight, and whenever I have strayed too far inland, I only have to glimpse the reflection of sunlight on water to feel at home again.

Simon Kirwan

Right: Wolf Fell, Forest of Bowland

Cheshire, the Wirral
& Manchester

Characterised by its geological features of red sandstone and long, golden sandy beaches, the Wirral peninsula is an environment of natural beauty, wildlife and small picturesque villages. Surrounded by the river Dee to the south, the river Mersey to the north, and the Irish Sea to the west, the area has its own distinct identity and a rich cultural history. Along with the neighbouring county of Cheshire, the region is a rural haven with areas of international ecological importance. From the dense woodland of Delamere to the craggy, coastal hillside of Thurstaston, it can almost be seen as England in miniature. The three small Hilbre Islands in the Dee estuary, just off the coast at West Kirby, are a fine example of the area's unique appeal. A safe haven for migratory birds, it also has its own colony of inquisitive grey seals.

Hilbre *right*

Hilbre is the largest of a group of three tidal islands that lie at the mouth of the Dee estuary. The islands are cut off from the mainland by the tide for up to five hours out of every 12; it is thought that these rocky outcrops were part of the mainland until the end of the last ice age, when melting ice led to increased water levels. The islands are an important stopping-off point for migrating birds; the Hilbre Island bird observatory was established in 1957 to monitor migration patterns. There are also large numbers of grey seals who regularly visit Hilbre, while dolphins and porpoises have been occasionally sighted in the waters around the islands. Apart from the wildlife, the Dee Estuary ranger is now the only permanent resident on Hilbre.

Middle Eye

Middle Eye, along with Little Eye and Hilbre, has been designated as a local nature reserve and forms part of the Dee Estuary Site of Special Scientific Interest. Sometimes known as Little Hilbre, the island is only 3 acres across; this grass-covered sandstone outcrop is an important high water roosting site for ducks and wading birds. Volunteer wardens ensure that visitors enjoy the island's beauty without disturbing the fragile habitat of wildflowers, crustaceans and rare birds.

Little Eye

The smallest of the three Hilbre Islands, Little Eye is the first reached when walking from the mainland at West Kirby and is less than half an acre in size. The glorious red rock from which the islands are formed is Bunter Sandstone, which can also be found on the mainland forming a rocky ridge down to Thurstaston. With the land around the islands alternating between submersion by sea water

and exposure, the rocky shores have a unique mix of plants and animal species that can best adapt to these extreme conditions. This also provides for a rich source of food for the waders who visit the area.

Thurstaston

An area of particular interest to geologists, the Wirral peninsula is characterised by red sandstone, which for the most part is overlain by a layer of boulder clay up to 100ft (30m) thick in places. Many of the pebbles and small boulders that litter the beach were brought to the area by melting glaciers during the last ice age and can be traced from as far away as the Lake District and Scotland. The wide variety of terrain at Thurstaston (between West Kirby and Heswall) provides a range of habitats for flora and fauna alike. Close to the beach, wildflowers such as these oxeye daisies thrive on the grassy hillocks, which throughout the summer months are ablaze with colour. Looking out across the Dee estuary, the Clwydian Hills of north Wales can be seen clearly in the distance.

Thurstaston Hill

This modest hill is just 255ft (90m) above sea-level but from its summit visitors can enjoy one of the best views across the Wirral and the Dee estuary. On a clear day both the Liverpool cathedrals, Blackpool Tower, Formby Point, the Clwydian Hills and the north Wales coast, and even the Snowdonia National Park, are visible. Thurstaston is home to a large red stone outcrop known locally as Thor's Stone. Some say the stone was raised by the Danes to commemorate a great battle, while others suggest it was the site of ritual sacrifices made to Thor by the Vikings. The Vikings certainly settled across this area and may well have celebrated their rituals here, but the more likely explanation is that this unusual outcrop is simply a glacial erratic.

Parkgate

At one time Parkgate, just north of Neston, was a popular seaside resort and one of the main departure points for ships sailing to Ireland. However, the progressive silting of the Dee estuary saw the town's sands become consumed by grass and, with no access to the beach, the once fashionable resort fell into decline. During the Second World War, decoy lights were placed across the marshes here to confuse German bombers into thinking they were heavily-populated settlements. Nowadays, the marshes are part of an RSPB nature reserve.

Stretton

Built in the 17th century, Stretton Watermill, south of Chester, is a small mill in the heart of the picturesque Cheshire countryside. The site has been used for corn-milling since as early as 1351, and it remained in use for the commercial production of flour until the retirement of the last miller in 1959. The building has since been restored as a working museum and visitors can see the two waterwheels driving the ancient wooden mill machinery and turning the millstones.

Beeston Castle

Perched majestically atop Beeston Crag, the striking ruins of Beeston Castle stand at over 500ft (152m) on an outcrop of red sandstone. The origins of the building date back to 1226, when Ranulf, Earl of Chester, decided to build an impregnable fortress to defend the Welsh border. The castle design is, unusually for an English castle, of Saracen influence, possibly due to the fact that Ranulf spent time in Syria during the Crusades. Aside from the natural defences provided by the steep hill, it was extremely well fortified. It fell into disrepair during the 16th century but, with the outbreak of the Civil War, it was quickly brought back into use as a Royalist stronghold.

Frodsham

Looking down onto the small market town of Frodsham, the horizon is dominated by the cooling towers of Fiddlers Ferry power station. One of its eight towers collapsed in January 1984, due to the freak high winds of that winter, but it has since been rebuilt. The raking M56 motorway viaduct dissects the landscape, separating the red-bricked residential area from the oil and chemical industries to the west. The river Weaver flows through the outskirts of the town and into the estuary of the river Mersey. In the 19th century much of the land surrounding the town was marsh and it is this drained area that has provided land for agricultural and industrial use. The town nestles in the shelter of Overton Hill, which at one time was a popular destination for visitors from Liverpool and the surrounding area. The "Overton pleasure grounds" had tea shops, fairground attractions and donkey rides and were famous throughout the region.

Delamere Forest

Delamere Forest Park comprises over 2,345 acres of open grasslands, wetlands and mixed deciduous and evergreen forest. Its name derives from the Norman period, from the French for "forest of the meres". The forest is the remaining fragment of the great Norman forest of Mara and Mondrum, used for hunting by the Earls of Chester. At its heart is Blakemere Moss, the Forestry Commission's largest wetland reclamation site. Between 1793-1815 the area was drained and planted with trees to provide timber for shipbuilding, but the Forestry Commission has now removed the trees and is allowing the area to re-flood naturally. As a result, it has become an internationally recognised Site of Special Scientific Interest. A haven for birds and insects, the forest has a wide variety of wildlife within its distinct and varied habitats.

Its six waymarked paths make Delamere Forest popular with walkers and cyclists alike. Lying within the forest is Black Lake, with its floating raft of vegetation and large population of dragonflies, and the mysterious Blakemere Moss. This eerie wetland, with its felled trees floating in the naturally re-flooded waters, creates an image of the land that time forgot. Although it was through human intervention that this land was drained and subsequently planted with woodland, it is fitting that this seemingly natural landscape has been re-created through a desire to restore the forest to its rightful state. By autumn, the greenery of the forest's many larch and beech trees will be spectacularly transformed into rich warm tones of gold.

Salford Quays

The bold glass and metallic structures that rise from the old docklands embody the regeneration that has taken place in Salford Quays. With an eclectic mix of bars, cafes, restaurants, shops and cultural attractions, the once derelict waterfront has been transformed beyond all recognition, turning a wasteland into a major tourist attraction. The success of this development has led to the fastest drop in unemployment in the Greater Manchester region and, amazingly, more people now work on the site than in its heyday as a seaport. The Victoria Harbour Building shown here exemplifies how the modern Quays complement the historic waterfront of the old docklands. Located at the heart of the redevelopment of Salford Quays, the Lowry Centre has given a home to creativity, entertainment and the performing arts.

Manchester Central Library

In the first rank of the city's most recognisable and famous landmarks, Manchester's Central Library is one of the largest lending and reference libraries outside London. Designed by the architect E Vincent Harris, the foundation stone was laid in 1930 by the Prime Minister Ramsay MacDonald and building work was completed four years later. This wonderful aerial view of the building allows a rare glimpse of the large domed glass roof which covers the central reading room, a feature obscured from street level by the higher surrounding lead-covered roof.

The Lowry Footbridge

The centrepiece of Salford Quays is the spectacular lifting footbridge which spans the Manchester Ship Canal and links the Lowry Centre with Trafford Wharfside and the site of the Imperial War Museum North. Completed in June 1999, the 300ft (92m) long bridge provides pedestrian and cycle access across the canal while continuing to allow the flow of shipping, thanks to a vertical lifting design which raises the bridge 75ft (23m).

West Lancashire, Fylde & Merseyside

There can be few places with such a wide range of scenery and terrain as this region of Lancashire. From the hustle and bustle of the seaside towns of Blackpool and Southport to the tranquillity of small villages and inland waterways it is an area of constant change and surprise. As the flat coastal land rises up into the West Lancashire hills, the region can perhaps best be appreciated from the top of Parbold Hill. Here the view to the west takes in the coast out towards Southport and the Irish Sea or turn to the north and look out over High Moor (right) and the rolling West Lancashire plains. Near the summit of Parbold Hill stands the Parbold Bottle (below), a stone monument which was built to celebrate the passing of the Reform Act in 1832. The structure was rebuilt in 1958.

Parbold

From the flat coastal plain of south-west Lancashire, Parbold Hill rises sharply to 400ft (123m) above sea level. It offers wonderful views of the surrounding area and is also a fine starting point for a walk through an area of trees and woodland known locally as "The Fairy Glen". Under a canopy of leaves and branches, tranquillity and beauty abound, rewarding the walker at every turn. This delightful glade remains one of Lancashire's hidden treasures.

Glasson Dock

Although today it is a busy port and yachting marina, just over 200 years ago the area where the village of Glasson Dock now stands would have been little more than rough pasture and wetlands. When the larger shipping vessels found that navigation through the shallow waters of the Lune Channel into the Lancaster Quays was becoming increasingly difficult, Parliament instructed the Port Commission to remedy the problem. By 1779 the Commission decided to build a wet dock at Glasson and by 1787 the first ship, the *Mary*, docked at the newly created Glasson Dock. By 1834, with a small village community now developed around the dock, Glasson's first shipyard was opened, along with other port buildings including a Customs House and Watch House. A branch railway to Lancaster followed shortly afterwards; now closed, today it is a well-liked walking and cycle route. While Glasson Dock is a popular visitor attraction, it remains a thriving working dock. It handles over 150,000 tonnes of cargo annually, shipping out coal to the Isle of Man and the Outer Hebrides while handling the inward traffic of fertiliser and animal foodstuffs.

Pilling

The village of Pilling is located on the northern coast of the Fylde peninsula between Fleetwood and Lancaster. Until the 1830s, when the surrounding bog was reclaimed, it was an isolated community. In fact, the name Pilling itself means "creek" and the original settlement was essentially an island. It is separated from the Irish Sea by an extensive area of marsh and mossland which provides a unique habitat for plants and wildlife and is regarded as one of the region's premier birdwatching sites. The once extensive panorama of lowland bog led to a local saying that "God's Grace and Pilling Moss are endless". An abandoned car, rotting in the wash on Pilling Sands, serves as a reminder that not everyone respects this fragile environment.

Skippool

Once a lively port, nowadays, when the tide is out, Skippool is more like a shanty town than the sort of place one normally associates with the sailing fraternity. Ramshackle jetties and assorted nautical craft in varying states of repair are tethered to the moorings at Skippool Creek. The rather sad and forlon looking fishing vessel (above) is now just a rotting hulk of rust and timber, seemingly waiting to be swamped once and for all by the incoming tide.

Skippool history

In the 18th century, before the rise of Glasson Dock and Fleetwood, Skippool was one of two docks serving the town of Poulton – the other was at Wardleys in Hambleton on the north side of the river.

Skippool

At one time, ships from Russia and Barbados would unload their exotic cargoes of wine, sugar, rum and tobacco at Skippool. In fact, by the middle of the 18th century, the volume of traffic at Skippool and Wardleys is believed to have exceeded that of Liverpool. In its heyday, Skippool was a typical maritime town, with smuggling and press gangs, contraband, spirits and drunken mariners. Skippool's demise as a busy port came with the emergence of the port at neaby Fleetwood, which, with its railway and ability to handle larger ships, rendered Skippool obsolete.

Access to Skippool Creek is via the Wyre road where there is a car park and, beyond, a footpath along the southern bank of the Wyre estuary towards the yacht club and the Wyre Ecology Centre at Stannah. The entire estuary, from Shard Bridge, just south of Skippool, to Fleetwood on the coast, has been designated as the Wyre Estuary Country Park and contains an extensive network of country paths, nature trails, bird hides and riverside walks.

Blackpool

The Golden Mile at Blackpool is the stretch of promenade between the town's North and Central Piers and it has been a magnet for holidaymakers and day-trippers since the late 19th century. The advent of the railways enabled the factory workers of Lancashire to descend on the town during the traditional "wakes weeks" and swap the grime of industrial cotton towns for clean air and seaside fun. With its Winter Gardens, Pleasure Beach and Tower, Blackpool was able to cater for the needs of up to 250,000 visitors at a time. The Tower itself, at 519ft (158m) tall, was inspired by the Eiffel Tower in Paris and cost £42,000 to construct; it first opened to the public on 14 May 1894. A Grade 1 listed building, it is normally painted dark red but for its centenary celebrations in 1994 it was painted gold.

Jack Scout

Jack Scout is a limestone headland near Morecambe Bay, giving superb views of the Lakeland Fells. It is a popular site with visitors as it has good coastal access and is an excellent point to watch the Bore, the wall of water that signifies the advance of the tide rushing up the channel to fill the bay. In 1983, Jack Scout became the first part of the Lancashire coast to be acquired by the National Trust.

Silverdale

Home to a wide variety of plants and wildlife, Silverdale is an area of unique natural beauty on the north-west Lancashire coast. It is protected by the National Trust and the RSPB and offers wonderful views across the bay to Cumbria. The chimney (left) harks back to the area's industrial past and is the remains of an old copper smelting mill. The Victorian novelist Elizabeth Gaskell spent a great deal of time walking the coast at Silverdale and many of her readers believe she based her novel *Cranford* on the nearby market town of Carnforth. This literary connection is echoed in the naming of Silverdale's village hall as Gaskell Hall.

Jenny Brown's Point

Just south of the village of Silverdale lies Jenny Brown's Point, and from here there are splendid panoramic views south across the bay from Clougha all the way round to Black Combe in Cumbria. Morecambe, Lancaster and Heysham are all visible on clear days. Like many of the region's isolated corners, this fascinating area of shoreline with its coastal lagoons and saltmarsh offers an excellent habitat for a wide variety of birds and mammals. The origins of the unusual place name are said to relate to the story of a local woman, a nanny called Jenny Brown, who drowned while trying to save her children.

Lytham St Anne's

Built in 1805 on what is now Lytham Green, the windmill, which is close to the promenade, is the town's most famous landmark. One of several mills on the Fylde, it was fully operational until 1919 when a fire destroyed most of the internal workings. Rebuilt and renovated, nowadays the mill houses a museum chronicling the history of the building. Next door is the old Lytham Lifeboat House, which is now the Lifeboat Museum. The Shipwrecked Mariners Society were responsible for the first lifeboat stationed at Lytham in 1851 and, in the years since, the lifeboats at Lytham have been responsible for saving hundreds of lives. Lytham lifeboat is famous for its rescue, in December 1886, of the crew of the *Mexico*, following two disastrous attempts by Southport and St Anne's lifeboats. In the RNLI's worst tragedy the entire St Anne's crew were lost, while all but two members of the Southport boat perished.

Rufford

At the West Lancashire village of Rufford, the Rufford branch of the Leeds & Liverpool Canal breaks away to join up with the river Douglas; it is regarded as one of the most beautiful sections of the region's waterways. Also known as the Lower Douglas Navigation, this 11-mile stretch of canal runs from Burscough Bridge to the river Ribble estuary. The popularity of this stretch of waterway is emphasised by the newly-built marina at Fettlers Wharf (left) which can accommodate nearly 100 boats. The lock at Rufford is one of seven well-preserved locks on this stretch that enable boats to navigate the changing terrain.

Ashurst Beacon

Ashurst Beacon was erected in 1798 by Sir William Ashurst as part of a Lancashire chain of signalling bonfires to form a communication link from Everton Beacon in Liverpool to Lancaster Castle. It was built specifically to warn of invasion by the French during the Napoleonic "scare", when Bonaparte was massing his troops at Boulogne. Ashurst Beacon is the highest point of the Upholland ridge, and on a clear day it is possible to see the national parks of Snowdonia, the Lake District, the Peak District and the Yorkshire Dales. The chain of beacons could be seen by ships on the Irish Sea and was a useful visual aid to navigation by seamen.

Haigh Hall

Surrounded by 250 acres of country park and woodland, Haigh Hall is a Grade II listed building dating back to 1840. Located just outside the village of Aspull the estate was built on the south-western slopes of the high ground that rises up from the Douglas Valley, and has commanding views of the surrounding area. The Haigh woodlands were laid out in the 1860s, giving work to unemployed Wiganers during the cotton famine caused by the American civil war. The hall was formerly the home of the Earl of Crawford and Balcarres but in 1947 the hall and its grounds were purchased by the then Wigan Corporation and remain in Council ownership to this day.

Halsall

The Leeds-Liverpool Canal winds its way through West Lancashire close to the small unspoilt village of Halsall, just outside Ormskirk. The walk along the towpath at this section of the canal is a particularly pleasant way to see the local area. The brightly painted narrow boats are moored at a popular spot with boaters, just yards away from The Saracen's Head, on the banks of the canal.

Mere Sands Wood nature reserve

Mere Sands Wood is a nature reserve near Rufford in West Lancashire owned and managed by the Wildlife Trust. The reserve covers 105 acres and is made up of lakes, mature woodland, heaths and wet, sandy meadows and is served by three nature trails. Each of these trails passes through a section of the site that best represents one of the three key characteristics of Mere, Sands and Wood. Thanks to the careful management of the reserve, a variety of quality habitats for wildlife have been established, making the area particularly important for wintering wildfowl. Birds that breed in the woodland include sparrowhawk, kingfisher, great spotted woodpecker, treecreeper, and redpoll alongside the common tit and warbler species. In all, over 170 bird species have been seen on the reserve, and of these 60 are known to have bred.

Mere Sands attractions

The name "Mere Sands" dates back to medieval times when the area was on the shore of what was then England's largest lake, "Martin Mere". The lake was gradually drained for agriculture along with large areas of surrounding peatland. Lord Hesketh had the original woodland planted on the site during the mid-19th century and added rhododendron later. The management of the reserve is designed not only to encourage wildlife, but also to provide facilities for people to visit and enjoy the unique natural habitat. As well as being home to a variety of wildfowl, the reserve is of national importance for its wide array of dragonfly species. The area is also of international significance for its geology due to its relatively untouched layers of sand and peat. This warranted its designation as a Site of Special Scientific Interest in 1985.

Ribble

The long and winding river Ribble rises in the heart of North Yorkshire limestone and flows through the hills and valleys of Lancashire. It finally reaches the west coast and creates the estuary that lies between Southport and Blackpool. Regarded by many conservationists as the most important river estuary in the United Kingdom, it is the winter home to over a quarter of a million birds each year. In many ways the estuary remains a hidden treasure as the saltmarsh and mudflats at low tide may appear desolate and lifeless. However, the mud is the home to the burrowing creatures and insects that in turn provide food for the vast bird population. As winter temperatures rarely fall below freezing on the estuary the plentiful food supplies on the marshes and the flats in the depths of winter are vital.

Marshside & Banks

Marshside is renowned as one of the finest birdwatching sites in the country and has some of the best lowland wet grassland in the north-west of England, including habitats of swamp, saltmarsh and scrub. It is an important refuge in winter for pink-footed geese, wigeons, black-tailed godwits and golden plovers and in spring provides nesting places for lapwings, redshanks, shovelers and skylarks. The wide range of wildlife includes birds of prey such as peregrine and the short-eared owl, which can be seen hunting the area. The practice of allowing cattle to graze on the marshes in the summer months keeps the grass short and creates ideal conditions for nesting waders in the winter.

Just a few miles north-east of Southport lies the vast, untouched sands of Banks beach. This tranquil and distinctive expanse has recently been a destination for aircraft enthusiasts keen to see the test flights of Eurofighter jets from British Aerospace at Warton, just a short distance across the river Ribble estuary.

Marshside

The mudflats and sands that make up Marshside are situated at the southern outer shore of the Ribble estuary just outside Southport. Uncovered for the majority of the tidal cycle, and only covered by the sea for a very short time at high tide, the saltmarshes form an extremely valuable sea defence. More than 40,000 birds over-winter here and there is an RSPB reserve with bird hides and viewing screens for visitors.

Marshside was originally a district where fishermen lived; many of their cottages can still be seen today. As well as sea fishing, over the years locals have harvested shrimps, cockles and mussels from the muddy estuary.

Southport

Described as the "Paris of the North" and the "Jewel of the North-West", it was the arrival of the railway in 1848 that led to Southport's development as a traditional seaside town. With rail links to Liverpool and Manchester, Southport was able to cater for the many thousands of visitors who flocked from the Lancashire mill towns during traditional "wakes weeks". It owes much of its style to the Victorians who chose Southport as a destination for their rest and recuperation, believing as they did in the restorative powers of sea air and warm bathing. This era has left its architectural mark on the town from the pier stretching out to sea to the glass canopied shops and tree-lined streets. From the pier there is a view of the large expanse of sandy beaches and the Southport seafront including the newly built Marine Way Bridge. The resort is often joked about for having a tide that seemingly never comes in, and the beach was until recently recognised as a landing area for light aircraft.

Southport Pier

Built in 1860, Southport Pier has seen more than its share of incidents ranging from storm damage to fires to the threat of being pulled down by its owners. It was originally 3600ft (1097m) long but was extended in 1868 to 4380ft (1335m), but a fire in 1959 reduced it to its present length of 3650ft (1112m). However, it is still the second longest pier in the country, and the oldest iron pleasure pier in existence. By 1990, with the pier having fallen into disrepair, Sefton Council applied to have the Grade II listed structure demolished. It was saved due to the action of local pressure groups with a motion to demolish it being defeated by a single vote. Subsequently, sufficient funding was obtained to provide a £7m refurbishment, returning the pier to its former glory. In the evening sun, a view from the promenade shows the skeletal form of the Traumatizer rollercoaster at Southport's Pleasureland fairground dominating the skyline. Sadly, Pleasureland is no more, victim to changing tastes and competition from rival attractions. Its closure marked the end of nearly 100 years of fairgrounds in Southport.

Formby Point

Formby Point is a distinctive feature of the north-west coast, a tip of land jutting out to sea and marking the area where the Irish Sea channels into the Mersey Estuary. It was home to Britain's first lifeboat station from 1776 and the ruins of a later station built in 1809 are still evident on the beach. In fact, the road leading down to the beach is still called Lifeboat Road. Formby has England's largest undeveloped sand dune system and it is a vital habitat for a wide range of wildlife including sand lizards and natterjack toads. The most common dune plant is marram grass, or star grass as it is known locally, which serves a crucial role in holding the sand together and helps in the constant battle against coastal erosion. However, it is this very erosion that has caused a great deal of recent national interest in the golden sands of Formby beach. As layers of sediment are washed away, older layers are revealed and these have produced the footprints of people, cattle, deer, dogs and birds, thought to date back between 3,500 and 6,500 years.

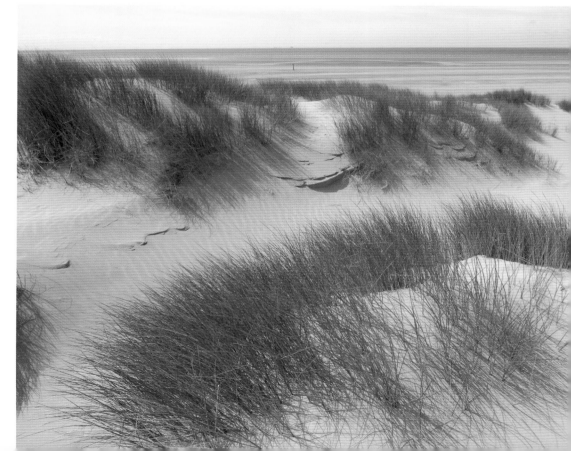

Formby

The National Trust-owned nature reserve at Formby includes a large area of the beach, dunes and adjoining pine forest. Although other stretches of this coastline have been reclaimed and developed the dunes here have remained untouched. Reaching a height of 65ft (20m) they form an essential barrier between land and sea. As part of their management, unobtrusive fencing is erected to encourage visitors to keep to selected paths in order to protect the dune system from erosion.

Liverpool Waterfront

When Prince Albert opened the Albert Dock in 1846 he was moved to say: "I have heard of the greatness of Liverpool but the reality far surpasses the expectation." How many thousands of sailors and passengers, when arriving in Liverpool for the first time, must have echoed those sentiments as they cast their gaze across the majestic facade of the city's waterfront? Its renowned skyline is defined by the presence of "The Three Graces", the group of buildings which dominate Liverpool's famous Pier Head. More correctly known as the Royal Liver Building (1908-1911), the Cunard Building (1915) and the Port of Liverpool Building (1907), it is perhaps the Liver Building which is most synonymous with Liverpool. Crowned with the city's famous Liver Birds, the clock faces of the Liver Building tower are actually bigger than those of Big Ben. The Jesse Hartley designed Albert Dock has come to symbolise the redevelopment of Liverpool, its restoration coming at a time when the city was undergoing one of the bleakest episodes in its history. From a derelict dock and warehouse area the site has been transformed into a vibrant tourist attraction and home to bars, restaurants and shops.

William Brown Street

Liverpool famously lays claim to more listed buildings than any other British city outside London and has more Georgian buildings than Bath. This fine architectural heritage is highlighted in the cultural quarter around William Brown Street, where the neo-classical buildings of Liverpool's World Museum and the adjacent Central Library

building sit opposite the magnificent St George's Hall and the Alfred Waterhouse-designed North Western Hotel. The hotel was opened in 1867 to serve the passengers using Liverpool's Lime Street station and its grand and imperious design complemented the adjacent terminus. It fell into disrepair but has now been restored and is once again a vibrant building as halls of residence to students of Liverpool John Moores University. Similarly, the World Museum, with its imposing Corinthian columns, reflects the 19th-century prosperity of Liverpool; it has recently been re-opened to the public following a £35m refurbishment. The museum's extensive collections cover archaeology, ethnology and the natural and physical sciences, a Natural History Centre and a free Planetarium.

In 2004, the City of Liverpool was granted World Heritage status. The area covered includes the Pier Head, the Albert and Stanley Docks, the commercial centre and the warehouses and merchants' houses of Duke Street.

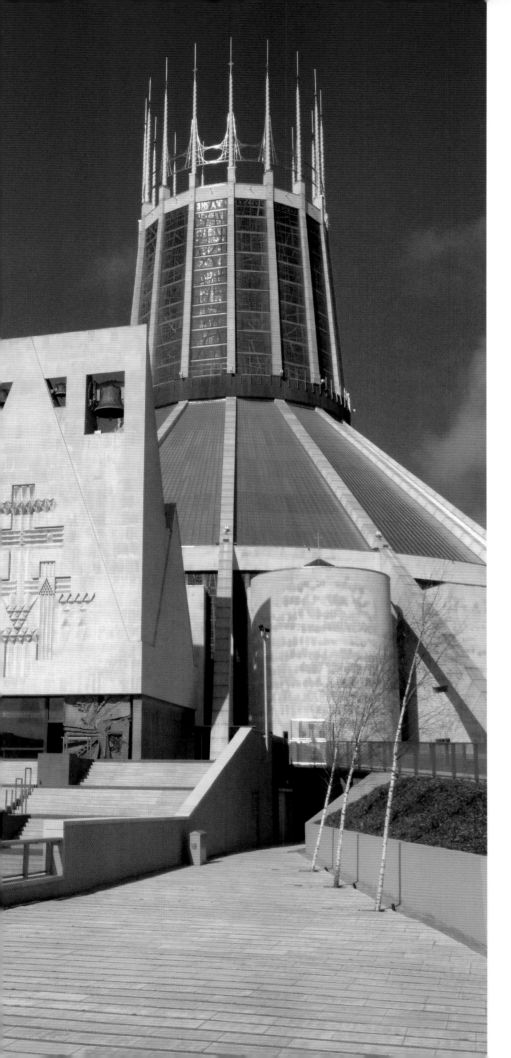

Liverpool Metropolitan Cathedral & Bluecoat Arts Centre

The unusual design of the Roman Catholic or Metropolitan Cathedral, coupled with Liverpool's strong Irish connections, has led the building to be affectionately known by locals as "Paddy's Wigwam". Originally, the building was to be a grand classical structure designed by Sir Edwin Lutyens, to mirror the neo-gothic Anglican cathedral at the opposite end of the aptly named Hope Street. However, financial restrictions led to the abandonment of this grandiose structure after completion of the crypt in 1941. Instead, the construction of this radical design by Sir Frederick Gibberd was undertaken, its circular shape allowing congregation and clergy to be more closely integrated. Just five years after building work started the Cathedral was completed and consecrated in May 1967.

Lying in the heart of Liverpool's retail quarter, the Bluecoat Chambers have become a popular meeting point and visitor attraction. Opened as a school in 1718, it is now the home of the Bluecoat Arts Centre and is the oldest building in Liverpool city centre with a fine cobbled courtyard, secret garden and Queen Anne-style architecture.

East Lancashire

Renowned by locals as Lancashire's hill country, east Lancashire is a region of relatively unsung beauty. From its series of reservoirs close to the West Pennine Moors to its thriving market towns further north, it is laced with heritage and history. Blessed with a unique landscape offering a multitude of habitats to a diverse range of wildlife, east Lancashire is an area of both national and international environmental importance. Seemingly dominated from all points by the imposing shadow of Pendle Hill, the area's stunning scenery sees leafy lanes meander through a combination of rural woodland and historic villages. At the northern edge of Pendle Hill lies the beautiful village of Downham, a rural idyll which remains unspoilt by the passing of time. Regarded by many as the most picturesque of all the Lancashire villages, it has been a popular location for film and television productions, most famously for the 1961 classic *Whistle Down The Wind*.

Pendle

Looking east from the summit, the Lower Ogden reservoir which supplies the majority of the drinking water to the Nelson area of Lancashire is clearly visible. It nestles within a large expanse of forest plantations covering over 50 acres and these have become a prime site for woodland birds. Alongside the more common visitors such as blackbirds and blue tits, the high-pitched trill of Europe's smallest breeding bird, the goldcrest, can often be heard high amongst the conifers.

Pendle Hill

The whale-backed form of Pendle was known to the Celts as simply "the Hill". Seven miles long and varying from one to three miles in width, Pendle rises to 1827ft (557m). From the summit, walkers are rewarded with a magnificent panorama, with views of the Lakeland fells some 60 miles away. Well-worn and established paths to the top of the hill make it a popular choice for fell-walkers and tourists alike, its dramatic appearance and mysterious history drawing visitors from far and wide.

The witches of Pendle

Of all the tales of alleged witchcraft in England, the case in the early 17th century of the so-called Pendle Witches is perhaps one of the most infamous events in Lancashire's history. In 1612, 10 men and women were tried and found guilty on trumped-up charges of witchcraft and murder in the Pendle Forest area. They were the victims of an era of superstition, persecution and a purge against the dark arts led by King James I (King James VI of Scotland, the son of Mary Queen of Scots), who lived in fear of rebellion and was obsessed by witchcraft. The 10 were hanged at Lancaster Castle after they made false confessions. Pendle Hill and the surrounding area remain closely associated with the witches and each Hallowe'en large numbers of visitors make the steep climb to the summit.

The Quaker movement

Mystery, myth and legend are closely entwined with Pendle Hill. In 1652, just 40 years after the trial of the witches, George Fox ascended the hill and claimed to have witnessed a great vision of God which led him to found the Quaker movement. According to Fox, he saw "the countryside alive with men, all moving to one place". Following his vision, Fox and other Quakers began to spread the word throughout the surrounding area. By the end of the 17th century the movement had spread throughout England and later to America. To this day, Pendle Hill remains a place of pilgrimage for the Quaker community worldwide, with followers tracing Fox's exact route to the summit.

Wards Reservoir

The mainly rural village of Belmont still has a reminder of the area's industrial past in the form of the local bleach works; the owners, the Belmont Bleaching and Dyeing Company, also own Wards Reservoir. Known locally as the Blue Lagoon, the reservoir lies on the north-east side of Winter Hill. North of the reservoir near the church is the Potato Pie Path. In the past villagers used this route to transport peat from the moors until landowners attempted to stop the practice by blocking the path. The outraged villagers held a sit-in for a week on the path itself. They were sustained by potato pies from supporters during the sit-in, until the landowners eventually withdrew their opposition.

Turton

Originally built during Tudor times, Turton Tower is a Grade I listed building situated close to the edge of the West Pennine Moors. At one time it was home to Sir Humphrey Chetham, the Lancashire treasurer for the Roundhead forces during the Civil War, and the tower itself was used for quartering troops. Set in beautiful woodlands, the distinctive 15th-century country house fell into decline during the Georgian era, but was lovingly restored and extended by the Kay family during the Victorian period. The nine acres of delightful gardens are home to an array of follies and a traditional English country garden. Today, the house features an outstanding collection of furniture, paintings and other artefacts dating from the Renaissance through to the present day.

Haslingden Grane

Located in the Rossendale district on the edge of the West Pennine Moors, Haslingden Grane contains three reservoirs built in the 1850s to supply drinking water to the growing industrial towns. The construction of Calf Hey, Ogden and Holden Wood reservoirs led to the displacement of the local villagers. Prior to the flooding of the valley, a community of 1,300 people lived in Haslingden Grane, which although mainly agricultural was also the centre of an illegal whisky distilling industry. Ruined cottages, abandoned farmsteads and old tracks all serve as a reminder of the people who once lived here.

Wayoh

Wayoh was built in 1876 as a back-up reservoir to ensure a continuous supply of water into Bradshaw Brook, vital to the running of the many bleach works in the area. Since 1962, thanks to the Wayoh Treatment Works, the reservoir has been used as part of the domestic supply to Bolton, providing up to 10 million gallons of drinking water per day. Wayoh is also an important home to a variety of plant species and many spots at the water's edge have been designated as Nature Conservation Areas and set aside as wildfowl refuges. The Armsgrove Viaduct carries the Bolton to Blackburn railway over the reservoir.

Jumbles

Once Wayoh was switched to domestic supply duties, construction work began on the 56 acre Jumbles Reservoir to protect the flow of water through Bradshaw Brook. On its completion in 1971, the Jumbles Country Park was opened, and it has proven to be a popular attraction for locals and tourists alike. Lying within the Bradshaw valley to the north of Bolton, the park is home to an abundance of plants and wildlife, with wild orchids thriving along the grassy banks. Jumbles itself takes its unusual name from a variation of "dumbles", a northern term for a valley with wooded sides down which tumbles a fast-flowing stream. To the south of the reservoir, amongst the silver birch and oak trees, Bradshaw Brook flows down though the valley, its clear waters washing over the stepping stone-like rocks.

Rivington Pike

A prominent point on the Rivington Moors at 1200ft (361m), Rivington Pike has long been used as a beacon point and was first recorded in use as far back as 1588. However, the tower that stands on the top of the pike now was built in 1733 as a shelter for grouse-shooting parties. Although no longer in use, and all entrances having been bricked up, it remains a Grade II listed building. The area was chosen as the location of mountain-bike events during the 2002 Commonwealth Games and is still popular with cyclists.

Rivington history

Viking raids and Norse immigration led to settlements being established throughout Lancashire, and it is thought that Rivington derives its name from the Norse "rowan-ton", meaning "village of the mountain ash". Its famed series of reservoirs were constructed as a result of the Liverpool Water Act of 1847 which allowed the city to seek water supplies from outside its own boundaries. The first of these was at Rivington Pike and despite opposition from local people, or "Antipikists", by 1857 the first water from Rivington flowed into Liverpool. As demand outstripped supply additional reservoirs were built at Anglezarke and Rivington creating what is often referred to as the Little Lake District. Today, in addition to providing domestic water supplies, the reservoirs are also a focus for recreation activities as well as supporting wintering wildfowl and wader populations.

Forest of Bowland

Often referred to as Lancashire's "hidden gem", the Forest of Bowland borders the Fylde coast to the west and the Yorkshire Dales to the east. An area of outstanding natural beauty, Bowland is characterised by its striking landscape of remote gritstone fells dissected by slender wooded valleys or cloughs which drain the vast tracts of heather-clad peat moorland. Steeply inclined walls of rock link the desolate high ground moors with the surrounding broad river valleys of the Ribble, Hodder, Wyre and Lune. The picturesque stone hamlets and villages are rich in history, and clues to Bowland's past can be seen throughout, from the Roman settlement at Ribchester, to the Saxon place names of Grindleton and Caton through to the Norse influences apparent in suffixes such as "beck", "gill" and "dale". Nowhere is history more evident than on the banks of the Ribble, where the weathered and crumbling stones are all that remain of the once magnificent Cistercian Abbey at Sawley, shadowed in the distance by the imposing silhouette of Pendle Hill.

Clougha Pike

Located in the north-western hills of the Forest of Bowland, five miles east of Lancaster, Clougha Pike's distinctive profile looms large over the surrounding area and presents a commanding view over the Lune estuary which lies south of the county town. It is visible from as far away as Barrow-in-Furness and the Old Man of Coniston. It gains its name from the series of deeply incised cloughs visible across its flanks. Clougha is part of an "access area" which, including the Wardstone and Tarnbook areas, covers some 1,717 acres of opened-up land. Access areas like this have provided large tracts of open countryside where walkers now have the freedom to roam the moors and fells. Although covered in part by large sections of blanket bog land, the fell is popular as a training ground with fell-runners, and each year the Darren Jones Clougha Pike race takes place across the hill. This challenging fell race covers five miles and includes 1400ft of tough slopes for the runners to ascend and descend.

Clougha Pike panorama

It is worth the climb of 1355ft (413m) to the summit of Clougha Pike to be presented with the spectacular view out over Morecambe Bay. Clougha Pike is the most westerly part of a wider range of hills including Grit Fell, Wolfhole Crag, White Hill, Fair Snape Fell and Wards Stone – Lancashire's highest point at 1840ft (561m). Together, they form a large horseshoe shape with the open end facing west over the Lune estuary.

The river Lune becomes tidal just before the historic city of Lancaster and meanders through a wide estuary passing Glasson Dock on its south bank just before it reaches the Irish Sea at Sunderland Point on the north shore. Britain's most famous artist, JMW Turner, visited the area; his painting the *Crook o' Lune* depicts a bend in the river at Caton, five miles upstream from Lancaster. Today many working artists have studios in Lunesdale and visitors can follow the Lunesdale Studio Trail to meet the artists and see their work.

Birk Bank

The Forest of Bowland boasts some of the finest grouse moors in Britain, and although the landscape may appear untouched, it is only through careful management of the fells that the population of grouse can be sustained. Situated on the edge of the Clougha access area, Birk Bank is typical of the Bowland fells with its distinctive carpet of heather. This provides feeding and nesting cover for the grouse, while benefiting other birds like the golden plover, curlew and hen harrier. The stone tower pictured provides a fine vantage point during the grouse season and is an ideal starting point for climbing Clougha Pike.

Forest of Bowland *(right)*

Much of Bowland is an area of open moorland which covers 312 square miles of rural Lancashire and north Yorkshire. The "forest" of its name is derived from the ancient meaning of a "royal hunting ground" and today much of the land still belongs to the Crown. In medieval times, wild boar, deer, wolves, wild cats and game roamed the forest, but nowadays it is the tranquillity and isolation of this untamed wilderness that define this most beautiful corner of north-west England. Scattered around the edge of the area are a collection of picturesque villages including Slaidburn, Chipping and Downham.

Longridge

Lying on the southern boundary of the Trough of Bowland, Longridge is a popular starting point for many fell walks. The fell itself stretches almost six miles, its gentle slopes sweeping up to provide a natural barrier between the Ribble valley and the Vale of Chipping. The summit of Longridge Fell affords panoramic views over the Forest of Bowland, the Hodder valley and the Pennine Hills.

River Hodder

The beautiful river Hodder is a major feature in the Forest of Bowland landscape. Rising on White Hill it flows for 30 miles before meeting the river Ribble close to Hurst Green. The meeting of the waters is an impressive sight, especially when both are in spate. The upper reaches of the river feed the large Stocks Reservoir, built in 1932, which provides much of the water supply to Lancashire.

Cromwell Bridge

Also known as Devil's Bridge, this ruined packhorse bridge on the Lower Hodder dates back to 1562 and was built by Sir Richard Shireburn to replace a 14th-century wooden bridge. It derives its name from the reported crossing by Oliver Cromwell during his march from Skipton to win the decisive Battle of Preston in 1648. It is said that Cromwell led his 4,000 men across the bridge in single file and it took almost a full day for the horses, mules and men to cross the bridge. Close by is the Lower Hodder bridge of 1819.

Stonyhurst College

In the shadow of Longridge Fell, the magnificent Jesuit College at Stonyhurst (established in 1794) is one of the most famous boarding and day schools in the country. As a Catholic institution in the 19th century part of the school's role was to educate older boys ("gentlemen philosophers" as they were called) who were prohibited by law from attending university. Stonyhurst counts Sherlock Holmes' creator Arthur Conan Doyle and the actor Charles Laughton amongst an illustrious list of former pupils. In 1648, when Oliver Cromwell stayed overnight at Stonyhurst prior to marching on Preston, legend has it that the Lord Protector and his troops slept on tables in their full body armour. With building work unfinished at the time, Cromwell pronounced it the finest "half house" he had ever seen. It is the second largest habitable building under one roof in England.

Slaidburn

In rural villages, the pub is often seen as the very hub of
the community. Nowhere is this more so than in the
historic village of Slaidburn where the local inn, the
Hark to Bounty, was also for many years the local
courtroom. Previously known as "the Dog", the inn
derives its unusual name from an incident in 1875,
concerning the village squire and his pack of hounds.
One hot day, whilst out hunting, he and his party called
at the inn for refreshments. Their conversation was
disturbed by a loud and prolonged yapping from the
pack outside. High above the din of the other hounds
could be heard the squire's favourite dog, which
prompted him to call out "Hark to Bounty!"

The village, situated where the Croasdale Brook joins
the river Hodder, is largely owned by one family and its
layout has changed little since the 19th century. Most of
the buildings are constructed from random limestone or
sandstone, using lime mortar to bind the rubble infill.
The magnificent 15th-century church of St Andrew is
situated on a mound near the centre of the village with
the elegant former grammar school nearby. At the lower
end of the village is a large stone barn bearing the
inscription: "Erected in AD 1852 for the use of the
industrious poor of the Township of Slaidburn, for ever".

Trough of Bowland

Lancashire's most renowned pass, the Trough of Bowland is a dramatic and narrow steep-sided valley that was formed as a glacial meltwater channel at the end of the last ice age. Although appearing untouched by human hand save for the working farmland across its rolling pastures, closer inspection reveals clues to the area's industrial heritage. Quarries, a smelting mill and a limekiln point to a time when Bowland was as much a part of the industrial revolution as the rest of Lancashire. The road from Dunsop Bridge to Lancaster through the Trough of Bowland is so direct that it is believed by many to originate from Roman times. It is also the only east-west road across the Forest of Bowland.

Ribchester

Over the centuries, the changing course of the river Ribble has all but covered the Roman fort at Ribchester. Located at a junction where the river converged with five major roads, *Bremetenacum Veteranorum,* as it was known to the Romans, consisted of both a fort and civilian village. It was strategically vital to the Romans in Britain, linking Manchester, Chester, Lancaster, York and Hadrian's Wall by road while providing access to the coast via the Ribble. The most significant remains are that of the bath house, discovered in 1837 and located just outside of what would have been the fort walls. There was also a temple, the stone pillars of which are said to form part of the entrance to Ribchester's White Bull Hotel. As the Latin name suggests, the fort would have been a home for veteran soldiers, retired from service who were allowed to farm in the area.

Wolf Fell

Wolves survived until the 17th century within the Forest of Bowland and their presence is reflected by place names such as "Wolf Hole Crag" and "Wolf Fell". Their favoured territory was the fell tops, while deer and game inhabited the lower slopes. Nowadays, the area is alive with walkers, taking advantage of the stunning views over neighbouring Parlick Fell and the picturesque village of Chipping to the south. The pastures of the Bowland Fells provided rich pickings for sheep and Chipping (an old English word meaning "market") became a centre for the wool trade and a market town for the local area. Many of its buildings date from the 17th century and, at the southern end of Windy Street, a carved stone on the former village school commemorates the cloth merchant John Brabin, one of the community's most notable benefactors. His name also appears on the gable end of one of the nearby terrace of stone-built almshouses, constructed from money he had gifted to the village. Chipping post office has the distinction of housing the oldest continually used shop in England.

Fairsnape Fell

Recent access agreements have opened up some 4800 acres of the most remote and unspoilt areas of the Forest of Bowland. You can wander over the rounded sheep-cropped hillsides of Fairsnape Fell or strike out over windswept heather moors where gaunt gritstone outcrops and black peat hags have been weathered into fantastic forms. People now have the right to roam freely over these areas, but as the land is privately owned it is still used by the owners for rough grazing, grouse shooting and water catchment. The by-laws and restrictions which are displayed on noticeboards at all car parks and access points must be observed.

Fairsnape Fell

The onset of winter transforms Fairsnape Fell, disguising its peaty wastes under a carpet of snow, with the trigpoint a stark monolith in splendid isolation. Trigpoints or "triangulation pillars" were originally used to enable cartographers to determine the exact shape of the country. They are generally located on the highest point in the area, so that there is a direct line of sight from one to the next enabling accurate bearings to be taken.

Parlick

Striding out over the spacious uplands of Parlick affords a stunning panorama of the surrounding Bowland Fells. Parlick's bog-free sides make it a favoured ascent for walkers, and at 1417ft (432m) high it is one of the most popular spots in the region for hang-gliders and parascenders who can regularly be seen using the Fell as a base for jumping. The summit is typical of the distinctive Bowland terrain of wild fell land, and the sense of desolation is heightened when the upper gritstone moorland becomes enveloped in snow.

Cumbria

Home to the Lake District national park and within it England's highest mountain, Scafell Pike (978ft /3209m), Cumbria contains arguably the most breathtaking and stunning scenery in England. A source of inspiration to poets, writers and artists alike, it is an area of wildly dramatic contrasts from tiny hamlets and villages with ancient stone bridges to lakes, tarns and craggy fells. Make the long and sometimes arduous climb to one of the region's many summits and you will be rewarded with unforgettable views like the one from the cairn at Pike O' Blisco (left). What better way to enjoy this unique scenery than from up on high, looking out onto the pyramid form of Bowfell and the surrounding fells?

Whinfell Forest

The Eden valley is an undiscovered corner of Cumbria. The river Eden rises at Mallerstang and flows into the Solway Firth north-west of Carlisle. The Settle to Carlisle railway follows the Eden valley, and yet it is unknown to all but a few discerning walkers. In the valley south-east of Penrith, in an often overlooked part of the Lake District, lies Whinfell Forest. This area of woodland, dense with Scots pine and Norwegian spruce, is a wildlife haven which abounds with a rich variety of flora and fauna. From the toadstools, wild mushrooms and heather that carpet the forest floor to the songs of cuckoos and bullfinches up high in the canopy of branches, Whinfell is full of delights and surprises at every turn. In 2004 a special red squirrel refuge was created in the forest, making Whinfell part of a vital network of conservation areas for these fascinating and much loved animals. This area will give the indigenous red squirrel protection from the ongoing threat of the non-native greys. The forest is also home to extremely rare floral species including the wild orchid Creeping Lady's Tresses (*Goodyera repens*).

Whinfell Lake

The most striking aspect of walking around the lake at Whinfell, aside from breathing in the fresh Cumbrian air, is the sensation of peaceful isolation. In the summer, the water-lilies that cover the surface of the lake enhance the beauty of this tranquil scene, adding another floral aspect to this already rich environment. Whinfell Lake is well renowned as a popular location for dinghy sailing and kayaking but the lakeside is also home to a variety of amphibians including rare species of newts, frogs and toads.

Arnside

Arnside sits on the estuary of the Kent river, where it meets Morecambe Bay near the Lancashire border. Its sands were famously crossed by Robert Bruce's men on their way to invade Lancashire in 1322. At one time Arnside was a bustling local port on the river with fishing fleets and mixed goods traffic of slate and pig iron. However, the building of the railway viaduct in 1857 caused the estuary to silt up, restricting shipping and transforming Arnside from a working coastal village to a holiday resort. From the promenade at Arnside there are stunning views across the estuary towards Grange and the peaks of the southern Lake District. The impressive viaduct was built by the Ulverston and Lancaster Railway Company; 1566ft (477m) long it is supported by 50 piers. Prior to the railway, the crossing of the bay relied upon an "over sands" coach service which ran from Ulverston to Lancaster. Today, you can still see vehicles using the sands, but nowadays they are the carts belonging to the inshore fishing and shrimping workers.

Easdale Tarn

Situated in an isolated valley in the central Lake District fells close to Grasmere, Easdale is one of the larger tarns in the Lake District. The walk to the lake from Grasmere is a popular route for novices and experienced fell-walkers alike. The poet Thomas de Quincey described the tarn as a "Chapel within a Cathedral" and such is the striking beauty of the view across to the east and the snow-covered tops of the higher fells it is difficult not to agree. With impressive crags on three sides there is very much a sense of being in the heart of the mountains. The tarn itself lies in a basin carved during the ice age by glaciers and is 70ft (21m) deep. Beneath its mirror-like waters, reflecting the blue of a winter sky, there is a variety of freshwater fish such as perch, eels and brown trout.

Easdale Tarn

Climb the well-established rocky path from the village of Grasmere and walkers are rewarded with constantly changing views and wonderful scenery. Following the stream adjacent to the path brings them up past the dramatic sight of the raging Sourmilk Gill waterfall. William Wordsworth and his sister Dorothy were constant visitors to Easdale Tarn and referred to the area as "the black quarter", blaming it for all the bad weather that hit their home village of Grasmere.

Fairfield

The Fairfield Horseshoe is one of the most famous of the classic Lake District "rounds" and this challenging walk takes in all the peaks that surround the tiny hamlet of Rydal. The majority of the Lake District peaks are visible from the broad, grassy summit of Fairfield which is widely regarded as one of the best places to view Helvellyn. Although a popular walk, it is one that should be undertaken in clear conditions as bad weather can make the route appear featureless and disorientating.

Fairfield Horseshoe

Climbing this horseshoe-shaped ridge is a challenge – it consists of a long and demanding walk with over 3000ft (914m) of overall ascent. Nook End Farm is the recognised start and end point for walking the Horseshoe. With well-defined paths for much of the route, navigation is assisted by following the drystone wall towards Hart Crag. A wonderful view at any time, the winter snow covering Nab Scar, the double top of Heron Pike and Great Rigg makes for an almost magical backdrop.

Wasdale

At 260ft (79m) Wast Water is the deepest lake in England. It lies in the remote Wasdale valley and at its deepest point is actually below sea level. Regarded by many as the most scenic of all the lakes, it presents a majestic panorama of the surrounding mountains of Red Pike, Kirk Fell, Great Gable and Scafell Pike. It is famous for the dramatic Wasdale Screes, a crumbling 1500ft (457m) high sheer wall of rock along the southern edge of the three-mile long lake. The nearby Wasdale Head Inn is a popular starting point for walks and climbs, and is often referred to as the birthplace of British climbing. Wast Water is the source of the river Irt which flows into the Irish Sea near Ravenglass.

The smallest church in England, St Olafs, is situated close to the hamlet of Wasdale Head and a stained-glass window in the church bears the inscription "I will lift up mine eyes unto the hills, from whence cometh my strength", a tribute to those climbers who have tackled the local peaks. The Wasdale Show is held in the adjoining fields every October.

Orrest Head

The writer and fell-walker Alfred Wainwright, famous for his series of handwritten illustrated guides to the Lake District, claimed his life was transformed by his first visit to Orrest Head. It is not difficult to imagine how such emotions would be evoked when presented with the stunning view of Windermere beneath the snow-capped fells of Coniston and Langdale. Such was the impression made by the view from Orrest Head, Wainwright felt moved to write: "Here, the promised land is seen in all its glory!" With the opening of the railway terminus at Windermere, day-trippers and holidaymakers descended upon the area from the industrial towns of Lancashire.

Eskdale Valley

Although there are several tarns on the higher ground, Eskdale is notable for being one of the few large valleys in the Lake District that does not have its own lake. The river Esk flows through the valley, water tumbling across its boulder-laden floor, all the way out to Ravenglass and into the Irish Sea. Looking east across the valley, one can see Hardknott Pass, the narrow and winding road that climbs to a height of 1289ft (393m), one of the steepest roads in Britain. Hardknott Roman Fort, near the top of the pass, provided commanding views for miles around and was the perfect point for the Romans to control the area. Continuing over Hardknott, the road becomes the Wrynose Pass, its unusual name meaning "pass of the stallion". At the summit of this pass is the Three Shire Stone, which marks the meeting point of Westmorland, Cumberland and Lancashire. Looking to the south-west, it also provides an excellent view out to the perfect mountain form of Harter Fell.

Grasmere

Lying in the valley of Rothay, the lake at Grasmere is relatively small, about a mile long, with its own, small, wooded island. A place particularly close to William Wordsworth's heart, he and his sister Dorothy are said to have regularly enjoyed picnics at this secluded spot. With its shallow, tree-lined grassy slopes, it is easy to see why he described it as "the loveliest spot that man hath ever found". There are rich descriptive names for many of the prominent features throughout the Lake District; looking up to Helm Crag one is presented with another example – the rocks at the summit here are known locally as "the Lion and the Lamb". From 1799 to 1808 the poet lived at Dove Cottage in the village of Grasmere; today the Wordsworth Museum is attached to the writer's former home.

Derwent Water

Known as "the Queen of the Lakes", Derwent Water is a three-mile long stretch of water with the popular town of Keswick at its northern end. With its wooded fells and tiny islands, and surrounded by some of the most magnificent scenery in the Lake District, it is a tranquil and peaceful lake with splendid shoreline walks.

Derwent Water is surrounded by some of the best-loved and well-known fells in the Lake District such as Skiddaw, Catbells and High Seat. The launch and boat landings, mirrored in the glass-like surface of the lake, are a perfect perch for the wildfowl and waders that populate the area.

Beautiful wooden launches ply the lake, starting from the Keswick boat landing and calling at six lakeshore jetties. It is also possible to hire a rowing boat or take a pleasure trip around the lake. There are splendid views of the fells and the many islands that grace Derwent Water including St Herbert's Island and Lord's Island, both of which are owned by the National Trust.

Ullswater

In the north-east of the region, Ullswater is the second largest lake in the Lake District at around 9 miles (14.5km) long and with an average depth of 200ft (60m). Some say it is the most beautiful lake in Britain, and it is often referred to as "the English Lucerne". Less crowded than the larger Windermere, Ullswater is extremely popular for sailing and there are anchorages and moorings dotted around its shoreline.

Ullswater attractions

The beautiful glass-like surface of Ullswater, accentuated by the stunning backdrop of mountain scenery, encapsulates many of the distinct features of the Lake District in one setting. The gently curving rocky shoreline of the lake combines with woodland and steep rock faces to form an idyllic Lakeland scene. Wordsworth was moved to compose his most famous poem *Daffodils* here after he and Dorothy discovered a myriad of the flowers in bloom close to the lake's edge at Glencoyne Bay. Now part of the area owned by the National Trust, this inspiring, daffodil-rich strip of land is known as Wordsworth Point. At the northern end of the lake lies the picturesque village of Pooley Bridge with its famous boathouse.

Rydal Water

At less than a mile long and the smallest of the region's lakes, Rydal Water is regarded by many as more of a tarn than a lake. Situated in the peaceful Rothay valley, it is connected to the neighbouring water of Grasmere by the river Rothay. Although surrounded by a number of popular fell walks, there is also a pleasant walk around the water's edge which takes in Dove Cottage, Rydal Cave and Wordsworth's Seat.

Thirlmere

Thirlmere, meaning "the lake with a gap", was originally two smaller stretches of water separated by a thin strip of land. These two natural lakes were known as Wythburn Water and Leathers Water. Extensive areas of lush woodland border the lake, much of which is accessible to the public. There is also an abundance of wildlife here including a colony of red squirrel.

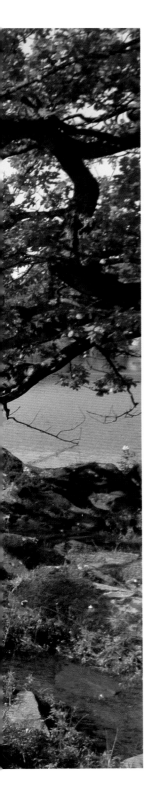

Thirlmere

The two small lakes at Thirlmere were much shallower than the modern lake, but the growth of industry in and around Manchester increased the demand for water. By the early 1890s Manchester Corporation had identified Thirlmere as a potential source for additional water and erected a dam at the northern end of the lake and flooded the valley. With the increased lake volume, the water was then supplied to the city via the 100-mile long Thirlmere Aqueduct. Access to the lake is easy, especially from the quieter minor road on its western shore. When the valley was flooded the settlements of Armboth and Wythburn were both submerged and the only remaining building is the beautiful small whitewashed church in the shadow of Helvellyn.

Brothers Water

At the northern end of the Kirkstone Pass, High Hartsop Dodd is mirrored in the glittering lake at Brothers Water which lies just south of the much larger Ullswater. Formerly known as Broad Water, Brothers Water is reputed to have aquired its present name during the 19th century when two brothers drowned there. A quiet and tranquil lake compared to some of its larger counterparts, the shallow, reed-filled waters are renowned locally for their rich stocks of trout and pike. The village of Hartsop is located near the north-eastern corner of the lake. In the past this was a busy settlement with mining, quarrying and milling. On its western shore is Hartsop Hall, a 16th-century farmhouse which is now owned by the National Trust.

Brothers Water

At one time Brothers Water was joined to nearby Ullswater, but over time silt has washed down from the fells and into the valley separating them into two distinct lakes. The two stretches of water, which are now approximately 2.5 miles apart, are linked by Goldrill Beck which runs into the southern end of Ullswater near St Patrick's Well. Dorothy Wordsworth described Brothers Water as "the glittering, lively lake". Today it is a great deal shallower and more reedy than at the time of the Wordsworths and there is debate as to whether it is the Lake District's smallest lake or its largest tarn. But its restricted size and the growth in vegetation is more than made up for by its location at the northern end of the Kirkstone Pass surrounded by glorious fells. Looking across the lake to the left of this picture, one can see Place Fell which rises to 2156ft (657m); it is worth a climb to its summit as it provides extensive views of the surrounding valleys and peaks and across the southern end of Ullswater.

Great Langdale

The Great Langdale valley and its dramatic rocky "pikes" are a great favourite with walkers and climbers. During the Neolithic period, the scree slopes of the Pike o' Stickle in Langdale were the site of a prehistoric "axe factory". The flint blades made from Langdale rock were traded across Britain and even today "reject" hand axes and fragments can be found on the slopes.

The Langdale Pikes

The most prominent of the Langdale Pikes are Pike o' Stickle, Harrison Stickle and Pavey Ark which are situated at the southern end of Lakeland's central ridge. Alfred Wainwright's own summary of the Pikes, that they are "once seen, never forgotten", is easy to agree with, not least because of the sense of scale they provide to the visitor. The Pikes' popularity lies in the wide variety of walks, from gentle climbs to technical scrambles. This view of the Pikes, looking across Stickle Tarn from near the dam, shows the rugged profile of Harrison Stickle and the steep rocky face of Pavey Ark. A popular scramble here is to ascend the 150m face of Pavey Ark via the challenging and notorious route of "Jack's Rake", a narrow path which traverses the face of the mountain.

Liverpool Bay

As the evening sun goes down over Liverpool Bay, the dramatically silhouetted form of the Lennox rig stands out from the horizon. This near-shore oil and gas exploration platform sits just five miles out to sea off Ainsdale on the north-west coast. Production from this field started in the late 1990s and the entire field has a gas capacity of the equivalent of 110,000 barrels of oil per day. The Lennox field is one of five offshore oil and gas fields in the Irish Sea. Oil is treated at the Douglas complex off the north Wales coast and then piped 10 miles to an oil storage barge ready for export by tankers. Although not as important for oil and gas production as the North Sea, the Irish Sea makes a significant contribution to UK energy reserves.